HOW TO HAVE A DAILY QUIET TIME

BY

E. A. JOHNSTON

ISBN: 979-8-9903273-5-1

Printed in the United States of America
June 2024

Formatting and Publishing by
The Old Paths Publications, Inc
11246 Oyster Bay Circle
New Port Richey, FL 34654
TOP@theoldpathspublications.com
www.theoldpathspublications.com

COVER PHOTO:

DEDICATION

The following study on the daily devotional time is hereby dedicated to the memory of my homiletical mentor and friend, Dr. Stephen F. Olford; who taught me the importance and necessity of the daily quiet time with God

TABLE OF CONTENTS

INTRODUCTION

Our walk with God is the most important aspect of our life: if we are remiss in maintaining an intimate love relationship with our Lord Jesus, then everything in our life suffers.

Unfortunately, many fail to take time to pray and to make time to study the Word of God—therefore many live in defeat and are spiritually undernourished. Statistics state that the average pastor only spends ten minutes a day in prayer. Ten minutes! If that is true, then how much time does the average believer actually spend engaged in vital prayer? Five minutes? Two minutes? Are our prayers self-focused to where all we do is ask for blessings and God's favor upon us and our families? Do we know anything about intercessory prayer? Or the real demands of costly, desperate prayer?

It is therefore a great priority to have a daily devotional time. This workbook will help the busy believer make time to pray and study God's Word and develop a regular habit of having a daily Quiet Time with God so one's walk with God is strengthened and deepened for further usefulness to God—for His glory!

CHAPTER ONE:

MARTHA IN HIS FACE,

MARY AT HIS FEET.

"If we are not living for Christ and eternity, what are we doing here?"

E. A. Johnston

In Luke's Gospel in chapter ten we read:

"Now it came to pass, as they went, that he entered into a certain village; and a certain woman named Martha received him into her house. And she had a sister called Mary, which also sat at

Jesus' feet, and heard his word. But Martha was encumbered about much serving and came to him, and said, "Lord, dost thou not care that my sister hath left me to serve alone? bid her therefore that she may help me. And Jesus answered and said unto her, Martha, Martha, thou art careful and troubled about many things: But one thing is needful: and Mary hath chosen that good part, which shall not be taken away from her" (Luke 10: 38-42).

Here in this striking passage of Scripture we find that Martha had a large meal to prepare for Jesus and His men. The text states, "as they went" meaning Jesus and the Twelve. Certainly, it was a daunting task to prepare a big meal on such short notice and Martha had every right to expect her sister Mary to help her in the kitchen. But we see from our passage that Martha's priorities were out of place. Not only that but she was bossing Jesus around! She was in His face! First, she questions Him: "Lord, dost thou not care that my sister hath left me to serve alone?" Then, she orders Jesus around! *"bid her therefore that she may help me."*

Clearly, sister Martha is agitated and consumed with getting the meal prepared over everything else. Her focus is on serving when her focus should be on Christ who is in her midst. Mary, on the other hand, sits at Jesus' feet to learn of Him. Her priorities are in balance. For worship must always precede service.

This passage reminds me of a story about George Whitefield, the great British evangelist. In 1740 Whitefield was staying at the Long Island home of Thomas

Fanning, a wealthy merchant. Having observed that his host was consumed with the material things of this world over the things of eternity; when rising in the morning George Whitefield took off his diamond ring and wrote on the bedroom pane of glass the following words:

"One thing is needful."

We must ask ourself the following question: "Am I spending enough time with God each day? Or am I too much like Martha, busy and encumbered about?"

In the next chapter we will deal with the priority of the daily quiet time.

CHAPTER TWO:

THE DAILY QUIET TIME

"God is looking for the Moses, who will take time to turn aside and encounter Him to experience change; so God can send him to deliver a nation."

E. A. Johnston

If you desire to go deeper with God and have a more personal knowledge of Him and His Book then establishing a daily devotional time is of the highest priority! How can we get to know someone if we do not spend time with them? When I first met my wife I could not wait to get in her presence to spend time with her and enjoy her company. So too, as we develop our walk with God we must spend quality time with Him.

My homiletical mentor, Dr. Stephen F. Olford taught me how to have a daily quiet time. But it was a stark statistic that got my attention! Dr. Olford had trained thousands of pastors from all over the world at his Institute for Biblical Preaching in Memphis, Tennessee. He shared with me a startling statistic: he had determined that in his dealings with pastors that the average pastor only spent ten minutes a day in prayer with God! Ten minutes! If that was true for ministers, how about the rest of the church members? Did they spend two minutes in prayer? I had to ask myself how much time was I spending with God each day in a daily devotional time with Him?

Where the rubber meets the road: please answer the following questions:

"How much time do I spend daily with God in prayer and bible study?"

1. 1Ten
Minutes___________________________
2. Five
Minutes___________________________
3. Two
Minutes___________________________
4. Longer, how much?________________

"Do I have the discipline of a daily quiet time with God?

1. No____ Yes ____
2. Can it be improved? _____________

CHAPTER THREE:

A DAILY HABIT

"Self is a tyrant that if not dethroned, will remained enthroned."

E. A. Johnston

In the study of developing habits it has been determined that it takes more than two months before a new behavior becomes automatic. Whether its honing a golf swing, or learning a musical instrument, time and practice become second nature to us. Establishing a daily devotional time is no different.

We must get in the habit of setting a priority first thing in the morning to get alone with our God. Distractions are our worst enemy. We must learn to put our phones on silent and find a quiet place in our home where we can get alone with

God. We must agree on a set time of day. This is critically important! For a devotional time to become regular there has to be a set time to be with God each day. Note, it does not have to take place first thing in the morning—some believers use the evening hours for their consistent time with God.

I myself was impacted by reading the account of pastor David Wilkerson, author of *"The Cross and the Switchblade"*. I was impressed by a facet in Wilkerson's life. Early in his ministry he was a country pastor who spent the hours of midnight to 2am watching television to unwind and relax. One evening God challenged Wilkerson to give that time to Him. Wilkerson sold his TV and never replaced it. From that point forward he gave God midnight to 2am, and it was during this time that God called Wilkerson to NYC to minister among teen gang members, eventually starting "Teen

Challenge." I realized that God did not reveal this wider ministry opportunity to Wilkerson until he chose to go deeper with God in a sacrificial daily quiet time. I had maintained a daily, regular quiet time for many years, but lately my time with the Lord was missing something—there was no "sacrifice" attending it. And the God of the Bible delights in sacrifice, for He sacrificed His only begotten Son for sinful man. After reading Wilkerson's story, I made a covenant with God to rise at 4:30am and give God the first hour and a half of each day—walking with Him. It is amazing how God has honored that time through the years! Leading me to ministry opportunities I never dreamed of!

1. "I will covenant with God to spend

____

2. with   Him   each   day."

____

(Please sign and date.)

CHAPTER FOUR:

HOW TO HAVE A DAILY QUIET TIME

"At the Bema Seat of Christ, will the fruit of my life as a believer end up as gold, silver, and precious stones; or will I stand there knee-deep in the ashes of a wasted life?"

E. A. Johnston

Now that you have established a time and place to have your regular devotional time, let's take a look at the pragmatic side of things you will need. As you begin your habit of a daily devotional time, try to refrain from "the lucky dip" where you randomly open your Bible to a passage to read. Rather, have a system of bible study and develop a pattern that works best for you. The key is to know the word of God better and to know better the God of the word!

Some helpful items to bring to the daily quiet time:

1. a pen to take notes,
2. a easy to read Bible,
3. a journal.

I have found it helpful through the years to keep a spiritual journal of my daily quiet time. At the top of the page is the date, and the biblical passage I am studying. In my journal I will jot down how I feel the Lord has spoken to me through His written Word that particular morning. I have filled up several spiritual journals through the years, and it has been helpful to get them out occasionally and see where I was at a particular time in my life, by reading how God was dealing with me at the time.

"I will go to a store this week and purchase a spiritual journal for my daily devotions and I will check task completed here when done"_________________________

I have found study Bibles to be helpful to me during my quiet time. I often rotate them. Through the years I have used the following three study Bibles during my morning devotional time:

1. Key Word Study Bible, also known as *THE HEBREW-GREEK KEY WORD STUDY BIBLE* By Spiros Zodhiates. This is a helpful tool for study of words in the original languages. It also has a Greek dictionary at the back.

2. *THOMPSON CHAIN REFERENCE BIBLE*. This helpful resource has an analytical and synthetic system of Bible study. I wore my first copy out and had to buy a new one!

3. *MATTHEW HENRY STUDY BIBLE*. George Whitefield read Matthew

Henry's Bible Commentary on his knees! This Bible has been my constant companion through the years as Matthew Henry's comments have stirred me and challenged me more than anyone else!

Whichever Bible you prefer to use, be sure to mark it up with a pen! Underline key passages that speak to you, highlight verses where God's Spirit speaks to you! A marked up Bible is a used Bible!

My daily quiet time articles checklist:

1. My pen___________
2. My Bible__________
3. My journal_______
4. Other________________________________

____

____

____

CHAPTER FIVE:

GOING DEEPER WITH GOD

"If you didn't live your life for eternity, you sure will have a long time to think about it."

E. A. Johnston

I was impressed by a story I read of an encounter between F. B. Myer and C. T. Studd. They were in America at a Christian conference and sharing a hotel room together. Each morning F. B. Myer noticed a peculiar trait of C. T. Studd while he was having his daily quiet time with the Lord. Finally, Myer asked him: "Why do you keep staring at the same Bible verse over and over again? Why don't you move on and read other verses?"

C. T. Studd replied, "I am meditating on a particular verse for a specific reason. I am memorizing the verse and asking God to make that verse a reality in my life!"

C. T. Studd knew the word of God and the God of the Word and he wanted to be saturated with the Word of God as a practical application in his life! He wanted change!

Is there a particular Bible verse that I would like the Lord to make a practical reality in my life?

1. Put verse here:

____

____

____

2. Do I want to go deeper with God? Yes___ No___

If we decide to go deeper with God, we must be prepared for greater usefulness as a result of our deepening faith. There is a sacrifice involved in going deeper with God, for what counts costs and what costs counts! This is true with anything worthwhile in life, whether its higher education or learning a particular craft. There is a sacrifice of TIME.

Are we willing to give up our favorite TV show and give that time to God? Are we willing to order our life so that most of our free time is spent on our knees and in our bibles? It is the miner who digs down deep who finds the mother lode--- everyone else is content with scratching the surface for just a few nuggets.

1. "How can I reorder my life to spend more time with God?"

   ____

   ____

   ____

2. "Do I have a sport or hobby that if I am honest with myself it takes up too much of my time?_______________

   ____

This was my own case with the game of golf. I got to where I was playing golf four times a week! Finally, God convicted me on my "golf addiction" by showing me one day what golf stood for from His perspective.

G O L F

Golden opportunities lost forever!

"Is there an area in my life that I need to turn over to God?"

CHAPTER SIX:

THE TEAR-STAINED GLOBE

"If God gave you an eraser, what part of your life would you erase?"

E. A. Johnston

"And Jesus came and spake unto them, saying, all power is given unto me in heaven and in earth. Go ye therefore, and teach all nations, baptizing them in the name of the Father, and of the Son, and of the Holy Ghost. Teaching them to observe all things whatsoever I have commanded you and, lo, I am with you always, even

unto the end of the world. Amen" (Matthew 28:18-20).

The Great Commission is the Mandate for the Church. Each of us should have a burden for missions and the spread of the gospel around the world.

In my daily quiet time for years I kept a world globe in my study where I had my daily devotional time. I would kneel and place my hands over a nation and pray for that nation. The next day, I would place my hands over another nation and pray for that nation. My hand would cover say, Africa, while I prayed for the nation of Africa and the spread of the gospel there. I'd place my hands on England, and pray for England. As I would pray I would weep in concern over the lost and perishing around the world.

I purchased a copy of "Operation World" which has each nation's church statistics and spiritual needs and I would read up on a particular nation and then pray for it by placing my hands on my globe. This is I did with regular consistency for years.

One day while I was in my study, the sunlight was shining on my globe and as I looked at it I noticed a peculiar aspect I had not noticed before. My globe was stained in several places with blotches—I realized these were stains from my tears. A tear-stained globe is a reminder of the need to pray for foreign missions.

I remember reading about Charles Finney describing his co-worker, Father Nash, whose life was given to prayer. Nash would accompany Finney to town and village and pray for revival and the salvation of souls. Charles Finney said, the last he heard of Father Nash was a letter he had received from him stating he was spending is days shut up in his room with a map of the world spread out upon the floor and Father Nash would weep and groan and pray over the world until he died giving himself to constant prayer!

    1. "I will buy a globe or a map for use in my daily quiet time to pray for the nations of the world."__________

CHAPTER SEVEN:

MANNA IN THE MORNING

"If you're not born from above and washed in the Blood, you'll bust Hell wide open when you die—even if you are the chairman of the deacons."

E. A. Johnston

I was at a weeklong Christian conference and busy everyday putting in long twelve hour days. When it was over I was physically exhausted. I went to my office the next morning without having a decent quiet time. I rushed my devotional time that particular morning and I was in the flesh and I sinned.

Oh, what a terrible drive home that day! I kept apologizing to God for sinning so carelessly! I asked, "Lord. How did that happen? I was on the mountain top all week in your presence and busy in your service then I carelessly sinned! How did that happen Lord?"

As I was driving a scripture passage came to my mind from Exodus chapter sixteen, about the Israelites and the manna. How they were instructed to eat their portion daily and not horde it for tomorrow.

> *"And Moses said, Let no man leave of it till the morning. Notwithstanding they hearkened not unto Moses, but some of them left of it until the morning, and it bred worms, and stank, and Moses was wroth with them"* (Exodus 16:19-20).

And as I was reflecting on that passage about the manna, it was if the Spirit of God said to me: "You cannot live today on yesterday's experience of Me! You must come to me fresh every day for your portion of Me."

I then realized the importance of the daily quiet time. How it must occur with regularity if I were to have a consistent walk with God. My prayer was:

"Lord, forgive me for not having a more consistent daily quiet time with You! Help me to develop consistency in my daily devotional time with Thee."

CHAPTER EIGHT:

ELEVATOR CHRISTIANITY

"If you've been suffering from 'Elevator Christianity', where one day you are up on the top floor of victory enjoying the penthouse suite, and the next day you are down in the dumps in the basement of defeat, then it's time to get off the elevator and climb the stairs."

E. A. Johnston

Have you ever noticed that at times the Christian walk is like an elevator? One day, you are on the top floor in the Penthouse Suite enjoying a life of victory and fellowship with God. Then, incredibly, the very next day down you go into the basement of defeat! Instead of a life of consistency it is more of an up and down recurring situation!

Maintaining a daily quiet time is crucial to maintain a close walk with God. In Amos 3:3 we read; "Can two walk together except they be agreed?" The answer is "no".

Having a life of victory is the normal Christian life. Not the up and down variety most experience. The Key to a Spirit filled life is learning how to live under the discipline of the Holy Spirit. I will share with you my notes from my homiletical mentor Dr. Stephen F. Olford on the Spirit filled life.

These are the conditions:

1. Holiness
2. Yieldedness
3. Prayerfulness

Dr. Olford's life verse was Galatians 2:20 which reflects the crucified life.

"I am crucified with Christ: nevertheless I live; yet not I, but Christ liveth in me: and the life which I now live in the flesh I live by the faith of the Son of God, who loved me, and gave himself for me."

Maintaining a regular daily quiet time in the power of the Holy Spirit will end "Elevator Christianity". Instead of that "up and down" existence, you will enjoy a life of consistency with Christ Jesus.

CHAPTER NINE:

THE GOLDEN HAMMER

"Jesus is my Faithful Friend but can He say that about me?"

E. A. Johnston

Having a daily quiet time can be enriched by understanding the keys to opening up the text of the Word of God. One must read the passage in question with three points in mind:

1. What is the historical principle?
2. What is the setting or historical background.

For example, the Book of Hosea is written against the backdrop of a time of spiritual declension in Israel. The Jews were experiencing a season of material prosperity under King Jeroboam II of Israel. But because of the practice of idolatry the people had become spiritually bankrupt. Hosea's call to repentance fell on deaf ears.

So the historical context must be considered as we study the text. Next, is the contextual principle. No verse or passage of Scripture should be interpreted out of context.

3. Next, is the grammatical principle. Every effort should be made to understand what the words mean as they were employed by the author.

Dr. Graham Scroggie employed a Bible study technique which he taught to my homiletical mentor, Dr. Stephen F. Olford who taught it to me. The Golden Hammer is a key technique to opening up a text of Scripture. Three questions must be answered:

1. What is the dominating theme?
2. What are the integrating thoughts?
3. What is the motivating thrust?

Using these key elements will help you to better analyze a passage of Scripture. When we determine the subject, structure, and substance of a passage it is much easier to understand. And this is where the Golden Hammer proves its worth!

CHAPTER TEN:

THE IMPORTANCE OF PRAYER

"Can our life be explained on normal terms or are we an astonishment to many?"

E. A. Johnston

The great British preacher, Charles Spurgeon, entertained a visitor one morning before church. The visitor was a young seminary student and Spurgeon asked the young man if he would like to see the engine of the church? The young man said he would. So Spurgeon escorted his visitor down several flights of stairs to the basement where his visitor imagined he was about to be shown the boiler room. Charles Spurgeon opened a set of double doors to reveal 300 deacons on their knees engaged in fervent prayer. With a wide grin Spurgeon pointed to the men and exclaimed, "Here now is the engine of the church!" If prayer is the engine of the church then it should be a primary focus.

The day the churches in our land discontinued the weekly prayer meeting was the day our churches ran out of gas. The importance of prayer cannot be more emphasized by the following Scripture:

> *"And in the morning, rising up a great while before day, he went out, and departed into a solitary place, and there prayed"* *(Mark 1:35).*

If Jesus, as the Son of God, had a desire to get up early to get alone with the Father to pray, should not that be our chief priority first thing in the morning? Most believers understand the necessity of a regular devotional time, but few put it into practice and make it a daily habit. Maintaining a daily quiet time should be our top priority!

CHAPTER ELEVEN:

THE IMPORTUNITY OF PRAYER

"When we are dead and gone will our memory be a fragrant aroma of Christ?"

E. A. Johnston

Often when we pray for a thing or a person, if we do not see immediate results we tend to cease praying. How many times in the past have we put someone on our prayer list and after a while removed their name, not because of answered prayer—but because of unanswered prayer. We often get discouraged and give up our efforts too soon. Jesus was very clear on the priority of importunity in prayer. Importunity is a big word and it means "persistence to the point of annoyance." This thought is seen in Jesus' story of the friend who wanted a loaf of bread. We see from the following passage in Luke's Gospel where Jesus was teaching His disciples how to pray:

"And he said unto them, Which of you shall have a friend, and shall go unto him at midnight, and say unto him, Friend, lend me three loaves; for a friend of mine in his journey is come to me, and I have nothing to set before him? And he from within shall answer and say, Trouble me not: the door is now shut, and my children are with me in bed: I cannot rise and give thee. I say unto you, Though he will not rise and give him, because he is his friend, yet because of his importunity he will rise and give him as

many as he needeth" (Luke 11:5-8).

The main emphasis in the story is the need was finally met because the friend had become so annoying at such a late hour and he would not take "no" for an answer, that the only way to get rid of him was to give him what he requested. This is how God the Father wants us to approach Him in prayer. He wants us to be persistent in our praying to the point of being a pest, so to speak!

Another lesson in prayer along these same lines was given to His disciples as He taught them about the parable of the "importunate widow". We read in Luke's Gospel the following:

"And he spake a parable unto them to this end, that men ought always to pray, and not to faint; Saying, There was in a city a judge, which feared not God, neither regarded man:

and there was a widow in that city; and she came unto him, saying, Avenge me of mine adversary. And he would not for a while: but afterward he said within himself, Though I fear not God, nor regard man; yet because this widow troubleth me, I will avenge her, lest by her continual coming she weary me" (Luke 18:1-5).

Once we develop a daily quiet time that is constant then we will develop our prayer life to be consistent as well—and that means adding the means of praying to God with importunity as we pester Him with our petitions!

CHAPTER TWELVE:

BEING AN INTERCESSOR

"The church today operates on money and manpower, but in former times it operated on prayer and Holy Ghost power."

E. A. Johnston

We desperately need intercessors today: men and women of prayer who will labor in prayer for our nation, for our cities, for our families. Few are willing to pay the price of intercession. What costs counts and what counts costs! Intercessory prayer has a cost of carrying a burden for the souls of men; a cost of hours of agonizing prayer on the behalf of "others".

We get a sense of what the duties of an intercessor are from the Book of Ezekiel in chapter twenty-two:

"The people of the land have used oppression, and exercised robbery, and have vexed the poor and needy: yea, they have oppressed the stranger wrongfully. And I sought for a man among them, that should make up the hedge, and stand in the gap before me for the land, that I should not destroy it: but I found none. Therefore have I poured out mine indignation upon them; I have consumed them with the fire of my wrath: their own way have I recompensed upon their heads, saith the LORD GOD" (Ezekiel 22: 29-31).

Sin had brought pollution upon the land and God was looking for a intercessor to "stand in the gap" between Almighty God and sinful man—but He found none willing to pay the sacrifice for such intercession. For true intercession is not only a commitment to prayer, but also a surrender to God's will in prayer! We have in our text the imagery of a hedge that is broken down and God is looking for a man to stand in the "hole" or "gap" to fill it. I used to live in a forest and I had a long winding wooden fence set all across my property of an acre and a half. If a board got loose, then dangerous animals, like coyotes and bobcats, could enter my property and be a threat to my family. As soon as I discovered a hole in my fence line I quickly repaired it! The gap had to be filled. So too, in intercessory prayer for our nation or for individuals we must pay the price of dutiful labor in constant prayer to see a victory. I will always remember the story of Rees Howell, known as "the intercessor", who prayed for the salvation of a son of a friend, and he prayed long and hard, fasting months at a time for the salvation of this young man. The victory came after several years of intercessory prayer!

At His most desperate time, the Son of God needed intercessors to pray among His disciples at Gethsemane. We see from the following:

"And they came to a place which was named Gethsemane: and he saith to his disciples Sit ye here, while I shall pray. And he taketh with him Peter and James and John, and began to be sore amazed, and to be very heavy; and saith unto them, My soul is exceeding sorrowful unto death: tarry ye here and watch. And he went forward

a little, and fell on the ground, and prayed that, if it were possible, the hour might pass from him. And he said, Abba, Father, all things are possible unto thee, take away this cup from me: nevertheless not what I will, but what thou wilt. And he cometh and findeth them sleeping, and saith unto Peter, Simon sleepest thou? couldest not watch one hour? Watch ye and pray, lest ye enter into temptation. The spirit truly is ready, but the flesh is weak"(Mark 14:32-38).

We must ask ourselves a burning question. Do we have loved ones who are lost? Are we making the sacrifice in intercessory prayer for them? Is our nation growing more wicked by the day? Do we take time and make time to pray for our nation? If the Lord in glory would look down upon mankind right now, would he find a man standing in the gap before Him for the land?

Answer honestly the following questions:

1. I have been remiss in my prayer life: Yes___No___.
2. I want to have a better and stronger prayer life for God and to become a true intercessor. (sign your name).

CHAPTER THIRTEEN: NEEDED PROPHETS

"Adrian Rogers made me think of Jesus. Every time I was with him I felt I was in the presence of Jesus. Who do you make people think of?"

E. A. Johnston

The greatest need in our Land today is a prophet. A man sent from God. God's man who will stand in the gap between heaven and earth, between mortal man and Almighty God. A holy man who is so wholly sold out to God, so intoxicated with Christ, and so consumed with eternity that his very footprints leave a smoky trail of the lingering fire of God. A man whose desperate life of prayer has left fingerprints on the horns of the altar in glory. A man whose emboldened faith and Enoch like walk with God moves mountains of resistance and proves that the God of the Bible is alive and interested in the most minute requests of men.

God will always raise up an Elijah whose prayers impact a sleeping nation. The Church in each generation has had individuals who live upon their knees, whose prayers reach heaven with a holy violence. India had her "praying Hyde"; China her John Sung; England her Puritans; Scotland her Covenanters; America her fiery E. M. Bounds; voices which gained the attention of the Throne-room, startled angels, and shook the gates of hell making even the demons quake and tremble with their desperate prayers.

CHAPTER FOURTEEN:

EMPTY OF SELF

"Are we willing to be decreased so Jesus can be increased in our life, or are we crowding Him out so we can be more visible?"

E. A. Johnston

R. A. Torrey once said, "If you want more of the Holy Spirit then He has to have more of you."

God builds His servants through His Divine process of reducing and decreasing. Gold must be reduced to its purity in the furnace of affliction. A branch must be pruned back with a sharp knife and decreased before it can grow more fruit. If we desire further usefulness to

God then we must submit both to the Refiner's fire and the Divine Pruning knife.

We must get to the place of absolute surrender, where we are willing to be reduced to nothing—so He can be everything though us.

Spending time with God in a daily quiet time will strengthen our faith, deepen our walk, and make us more and more like Jesus.

> *"But we all, with open face beholding as in a glass the glory of the Lord, are changed into the same image form glory to glory, even as by the Spirit of the Lord"* (2 Corinthians 3:18).

Answer the following questions honestly before God:

1. Do I have to always have first place in line or first grab at the turkey on Thanksgiving? Yes________no________

2. If I serve at church are my feelings hurt if I am not acknowledged for my efforts? _____yes _____no

3. Must I always be the center of attention? ___yes ___no

4. When I give money to spread the Gospel or give a love offering to the church, would I still give the same amount if it were anonymous? ___yes___no

5. Would I give to charity or church if there was no favorable tax deduction? ___yes ___no

CHAPTER FIFTEEN:

GETTING OUR PRIORITES RIGHT

"King Solomon was a man who had had it all, saw it all, and had done it all, and he was sick of it all—until he made God his all in all."

E. A. Johnston

The more time we spend with God in a daily quiet time the more direction we will have in life. God has a plan for each of us and it is up to us to discover it!

"For we are his workmanship, created in Christ Jesus unto good works, which God hath before ordained that we

should walk in them" (Ephesians 2:10).

God has a spiritual blueprint for each of our lives, our task is to find out what it entails and live it to the hilt for His glory! Then, when our life is done and we stand before Jesus at the Bema Seat for Believers, He will unfold that blueprint and measure it against our life and say "Just according to plan!"

King Solomon began well and ended poorly in regard to his walk with God. He allowed many foreign women to cloud his vision and he served their pagan idols. Life became futile to him, he surveyed it all and declared, "all is vanity!" His priorities were out of place, he had spent his life in pleasure seeking and he let the world capture his heart. Finally, he repented and turned back to God and the last words he wrote in his Book of Ecclesiastes was:

"Let us hear the conclusion of the whole matter. Fear God and keep his commandments, for this is the whole duty of man. For God shall bring every work into judgment, with every secret thing, whether it be good, or whether it be evil" (Ecclesiastes 12:13-14).

Years ago I had my priorities out of place in regard to my walk with God. Even though I was a Sunday School teacher at a big Baptist church, my free time was spent out on the golf course. I had been a junior golfer and was on my high school golf team and golf was always a big part of my life. But as I grew older and I was wanting to grow in my walk with God, I realized I was wasting too much time out on the golf course each week when I could have used that time to further the Gospel or strengthen my walk with God. Golf wasn't a bad thing and it certainly wasn't a sin—but was this good thing taking too much time away from God? I prayed about this until I got an answer from God. One day in my daily quiet time God spoke to me about my golf addiction. He said, "Do you know what golf stands for?"

I said, "no."

He said: "Golf stands for G O L F: GOLDEN OPPORTUNITIES LOST FOREVER

Enough said. I laid down my clubs and did not pick them up again for fifteen years.

1. Have I been guilty of having my priorities with God out of place? _________yes _________no. I can do better_______

2. What are some areas in my life that take too much time away from God and the furtherance of the Gospel?

____

____

____

CHAPTER SIXTEEN:

OUR GOSPEL WITNESS

"If there is a literal Hell that fills every minute with the damned, why are you wasting minutes by not spreading the Gospel in your community? What excuse will you give Jesus on That Day?"

E. A. Johnston

I have always loved reading Gospel tracts. I came to Christ savingly as a thirteen-year-old boy. Allow me to share my testimony with you. I grew up in a godless home where my parents always fought. My father was an agnostic, and my mother was a Catholic who seldom went to church and seldom read the big red Catholic bible that sat on the coffee table in the living room. On top of this, the house was haunted. A demon entity occupied the house we were renting. We would hear footsteps upstairs but no one was there—at least no one you could see. Occasionally, there would be a violent pounding on the hall closet door that would stop you in your tracks and send chills down your spine. One day, when I was home alone on a hot august day, the temperature outside was over 100 degrees and our window AC unit was not working. It was over 100 degrees in that house. I was walking down the hall when that pounding began on that hall closet door. Quickly I ran over to the door and grabbed the crystal door knob and jerked the door open as fast as I could. A cold blast of air, cold as a freezer, came out upon me and I never opened that door again. This was the turmoil in that little house when I was a young teenager.

My neighbor across the alley was a pastor and I went to school with his son. His son was an athlete at school and we had little in common and were not close friends. But this pastor saw a teenage boy in a troubled home and he began to pray for me. This pastor wouldn't let me go to Hell. He invited me over his house for breakfast with his family one morning. I sat at his kitchen table and he bowed his head and began to pray for each member of his family sitting there. He prayed for people overseas working in the gospel. He prayed for those who needed prayer in his congregation. Then before he stopped he prayed for me. That was the first time in my life I ever heard someone pray for me.

He offered me a job in his bible book store which was next to his house. It was my first job. I was thirteen. He taught me to do office work and how to sweep the floor with oil mop. But best of all he let me work in the front part of the store where there were racks and racks of bible tracts. I read every single one of those tracts. I delighted in the stories of far away places of sailors and pearl divers and explorers! And it was there working in that bible book store that I gained a love for gospel tracts.

For the last forty years I have handed out gospel tracts. I have given them to policemen and businessmen and strangers. I even wrote my own gospel tracts and paid to have them printed to hand them out as a gospel witness. A tract ministry is a powerful ministry if done on a regular basis. But I would have not known Christ at a young age had it not been for that pastor who had a burden for my soul and he wouldn't let me go to hell.

Let me ask you friend:

1. Do you have a tract ministry? ___yes ___no

2. Do you have a gospel outreach in your community? ___yes ___no.
3. What are you doing personally to fulfill Christ's mandate to all followers of His by His Great Commission:

> *"And he said unto them, Go, ye into all the world, and preach the gospel to every creature"* *(Mark 16:15).*

List the ways you are presently spreading the gospel:

____

____

____

____

____

____

____

____

____

____

CHAPTER SEVENTEEN:

ON FIRE FOR CHRIST

"If you end your days and you failed to risk everything for Christ and the Gospel, it will be too late then."

E. A. Johnston

We only get one go around in life. We can choose to live it for this present world and ourselves or we can choose to live it for Christ and the Gospel. We cannot have one foot with God and the other in the world. God will not honor a divided heart. Either we are "on fire" for Christ and living on the full stretch for God and His kingdom; or we are tepid Christians that just blend in with the world and make no difference in the world for

Jesus. Jesus said of the church at Laodecia:

"Because thou sayest, I am rich, and increased with goods, and have need of nothing: and knowest not that thou art wretched, and miserable, and poor, and blind, and naked. I counsel thee to buy of me gold tried in the fire, that thou mayest be rich; and white raiment, that thou mayest be clothed, and that the shame of thy nakedness do not appear: and anoint thine eyes with eye salve, that thou mayest see. As many as I live, I rebuke and chasten: be zealous therefore and repent" (Revelation 3:17-19).

One of the most miserable of persons is the believer who is lukewarm toward Jesus. Let me share a true story with you about the evangelist Duncan Campbell of Scotland. Duncan Campbell was used of God mightily in the Lewis Revival (1949-1952) on the Isle of Lewis in the Hebrides of Scotland. A revival gripped the island and it was said that the entire community was "saturated with the presence of God." Young people on the island were being saved left and right and turning their lives over to full time ministry. But before this occurred, Duncan Campbell had to pass through a "dark night of soul."

It happened one morning as he was in his study preparing a sermon for an upcoming minister's conference that he heard his sixteen-year-old daughter singing merrily downstairs. She was singing a hymn with fervor. Duncan Campbell put down his pen and walked down the stairs and he asked her: "Lassie, what are you singing about so early in the morning at six o'clock?"

She replied, "Oh Daddy! I just spent an hour with Jesus! Isn't Jesus wonderful Daddy!"

Duncan Campbell slowly turned and went back upstairs. He thought to himself: "Jesus isn't wonderful to me." "Here I am preparing a sermon on the Holy Spirit for a minister's convention and I cannot say right now that Jesus is wonderful to me!" This broke him. He locked the door of his study and threw himself on the floor. In desperation he sought God in prayer for several hours on his face and knees. His family thought he had gone mad! Finally, he got the victory! As he rose to his feet he could now say cheerfully that "Jesus was wonderful to me!" He left the settled pastorate and went out on faith as a missionary to the islands. And in one years' time he was in the midst of a glorious revival on the Isle of Lewis as the human instrument of God in revival!

1. Let me ask you friend. Can you say right now that "Jesus is wonderful to me"? ____yes ____no
2. Do you need a personal revival? ___yes ___no
3. Are you "on fire" for Christ and the Gospel? ___yes ___no

CHAPTER EIGHTEEN:

ONLY ONE LIFE

"God is looking for faith—He demands obedience."

E. A. Johnston

C. T. Studd, was born into wealth and privilege. His father was Edward Studd, a millionaire country gentleman who had made his fortune in British India, and his favorite pastime was racing thorough bred horses. One evening Edward Studd went to hear the evangelist D. L. Moody in London. Edward Studd sat listening to Moody and said to himself, "this man is telling me all about myself!" that evening he was remarkably brought to Christ. After that, his chauffeur said of Edward Studd: "He is a different man in the same skin." Edward Studd sold his race horses and turned his country estate into a place for preaching for visiting preachers. It was here that his son (the famous Cricketeer) C. T. Studd came to Christ. C. T. Studd gave away his entire inherited fortune to the cause of Christ and the Gospel and became a missionary to China, India, and Africa. He wrote the following little poem:

"Only one life

'twill soon be past;

Only what's done

For Christ will last."

The primary purpose of developing a deeper daily quiet time is to HEAR FROM GOD. Perhaps, God has a call on your life and you have not heard it because you have not spent enough quality time with Him. Get alone with God and get on your heart what God has on His heart—this can be done only through a developed daily quiet time with God. We have only one life: what are we doing with it?

CHAPTER NINETEEN:

BEING MARY AT HIS FEET

"A disciple means 'learner'. Jesus is Looking for those followers of His who are teachable."

E. A. Johnston

"And Mary hath chosen that good part, which shall not be taken away from her" (Luke 10:42).

One of the best ways to grow in our walk with the Lord is to learn how to apply what we have learned in our quiet time in a practical way in our daily life. Take the following verse of Scripture from Colossians:

"That ye might walk worthy of the Lord unto all pleasing, being fruitful in every good work, and increasing in the knowledge of God" (Colossians 1:10).

I asked the Lord to make this verse a reality in my life. There were four aspects mentioned in the text that I wanted to see become a practical reality in my daily walk with God. I wanted to walk worthy; I wanted to be pleasing to Him; I wanted to be more fruitful in my service to Him; and I wanted to increase in my knowledge of God. I sacrificially spent time with God in prayer, rising at 4:30 am to get alone with my Master. God answered my prayer to go deeper with Him. God was faithful to apply each of those principles into my daily living.

When we are like Mary at Jesus' feet we are both listeners and learners. We must pray over the passage we are reading to hear the Master's voice speak to us concerning His truth.

As we develop the regular habit of a daily quiet time we will strengthen our walk with God. Hopefully your daily time with the Lord is more regular than it was before you began this workbook.

If you have benefitted from this study on the daily quiet time then the next step is to introduce this study to your spouse or loved one so they too can strengthen their walk with God as they study His Word!

Let us say with the Psalmist: "I rejoice at thy word, as one that findeth great spoil" (Psalm 119:162).

CHAPTER TWENTY:

RECOMMENDED BOOKS ON PRAYER

"If Jesus held nothing back at Calvary to die for our sins, how can we hold anything back from Him?"

E. A. Johnston

The following suggested books have been of great personal benefit to me through the years. I highly recommend them!

1. *Preacher and Prayer* by E. M. Bounds (published by Old Paths Publications)
2. *The Pathway To Prayer* by Samuel Chadwick
3. *George Whitefield's Journal*

4. *David Brainerd's Diary*
5. *The Way of the Cross* by Gregory Mantle
6. *The Self Life for the Christ Life* by F. B. Myer
7. *Absolute Surrender* by Andrew Murray
8. *Bone of His Bone* by F. J. Heugel
9. *Born Crucified* by L. E. Maxwell
10. John Sung's *Diary by Levi*
11. *Memoirs* of Charles Finney
12. *Sam Jones A New Biography* by E. A. Johnston (Published by Old Paths Publications)
13. Rees Howells: *Intercessor* by Norman Grubb

No. 87. In the Garden.

C. A. M. C. AUSTIN MILES.

ABOUT THE AUTHOR

E.A. Johnston in the Outdoor pulpit at Hanham Mount where George Whitefield preached, courtesy of Digby James.

E. A. Johnston, Ph.D., D. B. S., is a Fellow with the Stephen Olford Institute for Biblical Preaching and is an evangelist and author with eighteen published books. He is the founder of Evangelism Awakening, a revival-based ministry whose focus is the study of historical revival and preaching for revival in our day. He has over two thousand sermons on SermonAudio.com.

SOME OF THE BOOKS BY E. A. JOHNSTON

Many of the following books may be purchased individually or as a set by going to Dr. Johnston's webpage in the bookstore at The Old Paths Publications that has links to distributors. Go to:

www.theoldpathspublications.com/Pages/Authors/Johnston.htm

1. *"A Heart Awake: The Authorized Biography of J. Sidlow Baxter"* Foreword by Adrian Rogers (The Old Paths Publications, www.theoldpathspublications.com).

2. *"Realities Of Revival"* Foreword by Stephen F. Olford (Gospel Folio Press, Canada; 2005).

3. *"No Turning Back"* (Gospel Folio Press, Canada; 2005).

4. *"The Master's Plan: Unfolding God's Blueprint For Your Life"* (Gospel Folio Press, Canada; 2006).

5. *"Know The Book: Bible Survey At A Glance"* (Gospel Folio Press, Canada; 2007).

6. *"Jua Kitabu: Tazamo la Biblia" Know The Book* translated into the Swahili by missionary G. I. Harlow (Everyday Publications, Canada; 2007).

7. *"Walking With God"* Foreword by Ted S. Rendall (Gospel Folio Press, Canada; 2007).

8. *"Return To Me: Entering A Right Relationship With God"* (Gospel Folio Press, Canada; 2007).

9. *"Are You In The Book Of Life?"* (Gospel Folio Press, Canada; 2008).

10. *"Call To Revival"* Foreword By Colin Peckham (Gospel Folio Press, Canada; 2008).

11. *"The Church In Revival"* Foreword By Richard Owen Roberts (Gospel Folio Press, Canada; 2008).

12. *"Olford On Scroggie: Stephen Olford's Notes on the Sermon Outlines of Graham Scroggie"* Co-authored with Stephen Olford (The Old Paths Publications: www.theoldpathspublications.com).

13. *"George Whitefield A Definitive Biography, Volumes 1 and 2 Combined"* (The Old Paths Publications: www.theoldpathspublications.com).

14. *"George Whitefield A Definitive Biography In Two Volumes"* (American

edition published by Revival Literature, Asheville; 2012).

15. *"God's Hitchhike Evangelist The Biography Of Rolfe Barnard"* Foreword By Bob Doom (The Old Paths Publications: www.theoldpathspublications.com).

16. *"Asahel Nettleton Revival Preacher"* Foreword By John Thornbury, Preface By Richard Owen Roberts (The Old Paths Publications: www.theoldpathspublications.com).

17. *"Sermons For Revival"* (The Old Paths Publications: www.theoldpathspublications.com).

18. *"A Noble Company Biographical Essays on Notable Particular Baptists in America Volume 11: Portrait of Rolfe Barnard"* (Particular Baptist Press, Springfield; 2018).

19. *"Lectures On Revival For A Laodicean Church,"* (The Old Paths

Publications,
www.theoldpathspublications.com)

20. *"Sam Jones, A New Biography"* (The Old Paths Publications: www.theoldpathspublications.com)

21. E. A. Johnston's Book Set, (The Old Paths Publications, www.theoldpathspublications.com (30% off retail)

Many of these books can be purchased in The Old Paths Publications Bookstore at a discounted price. Go here:

E. A. Johnston Books (theoldpathspublications.com)

or

https://www.theoldpathspublications.com/Pages/BookStore.htm

www.ingramcontent.com/pod-product-compliance
Lightning Source LLC
Chambersburg PA
CBHW061341140726
47997CB00003B/1033